UNTANGLED

A
step-by-step
guide to joy
and
success
for the modern
yarn lover

BY **SHELLEY BRANDER**

One of my favorite things about knitting and crocheting is that it's a lifelong journey. There's always more to learn and do! But it can also be overwhelming. It's hard to find people who love yarn as much as you do. Your stash can quickly grow beyond life expectancy! And without a clear path forward, it's easy to get mired in unfinished projects, unused stash and unrealized dreams.

In "Untangled," we've taken our 14+ years of experience helping other yarn lovers as:

- Loops (a local yarn store and online store) - loopslove.com
- LoopsLove Challenge (a global online challenge group) - loopsmembers.com
- LoopsClub (a luxury yarn kit club) - loopsmembers.com
- Knit Stars (a global online workshop event) - knitstars.com

...and we've distilled it all into a progressive series of fun workbook chapters. Work through the chapters in order, or skip around. You are the boss of your yarn, and there are no knitting police :)

We hope *Untangled* brings more clarity and joy to your own yarn journey.

XOXO,
Shelley

TABLE OF CONTENTS

CHAPTER

1

*The 21-Day Stitch
Every Day Challenge*

CHAPTER

2

*The 90-Day LoopsLove
Stash Challenge*

We've come to believe there are distinct stages to every yarn lover's journey.

WE CALL IT THE LOOPSLOVE SUCCESS PATH.

Each stage is fun and exciting! And just when you might become bored with one stage, it's time to push yourself to the next. **Which stage of the LoopsLove Success Path are you in right now?**

Mark your current stage, then periodically look back and track how far you've progressed.

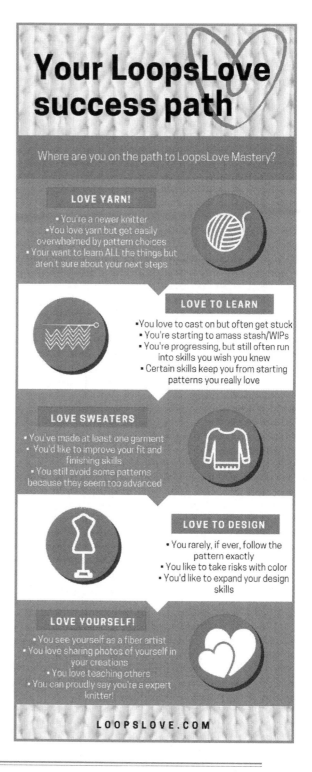

Your LoopsLove success path

Where are you on the path to LoopsLove Mastery?

LOVE YARN!
- You're a newer knitter
- You love yarn but get easily overwhelmed by pattern choices
- Your want to learn ALL the things but aren't sure about your next steps

LOVE TO LEARN
- You love to cast on but often get stuck
- You're starting to amass stash/WIPs
- You're progressing, but still often run into skills you wish you knew
- Certain skills keep you from starting patterns you really love

LOVE SWEATERS
- You've made at least one garment
- You'd like to improve your fit and finishing skills
- You still avoid some patterns because they seem too advanced

LOVE TO DESIGN
- You rarely, if ever, follow the pattern exactly
- You like to take risks with color
- You'd like to expand your design skills

LOVE YOURSELF!
- You see yourself as a fiber artist
- You love sharing photos of yourself in your creations
- You love teaching others
- You can proudly say you're a expert knitter!

LOOPSLOVE.COM

CHAPTER 1:

The 21-Day Stitch Every Day Challenge

INTRO:

Over the years of getting to know yarn lovers through Loops (our local yarn store), LoopsLove.com, LoopsClub.com and KnitStars.com...we've noticed a common denominator.

The happiest knitters are not necessarily the ones who knit the *fastest*.

Or the *fanciest*.

They're just the ones who knit the *most*.

They're the people who make it a priority to sit down, relax and really enjoy their craft – every day. Even if it's only a few stitches.

Whether you see yourself as a beginner...or a slow knitter...or someone who makes a lot of mistakes...or someone with too many works in progress...or someone who never finishes things...or someone with too much stash (um, that would be *all of us!*)...

This tiny commitment – to knit every day – can transform you into exactly the kind of knitter you long to be.

Knit every day, and you'll find yourself progressing. Finishing. Wearing. Giving. And most of all, loving every minute of it.

So we begin with this simplest of all challenges.

It's not a race.

It's not a competition.

It's just a framework for re-thinking the way you want to create, then building a habit, then living it.

Before you know it, you'll be living the LoopsLove Life. Let's go!

P.S. You can do this for 21 days or do it for a lifetime! The 21 is just our suggestion.

FIND YOUR BIG WHY.

Think back to why you started knitting or crocheting. Reflect on how you feel when you are in the "knitting zone," really enjoying a project.

I knit because...

I want to knit more often because...

ACTION ITEM:

☐ Take a moment to share your big why
in the LoopsLove Challenge Facebook Group http://bit.ly/loops-love

CREATE YOUR PERFECT KNITTING SPACE.

Next, take some time to "feather your knitting nest." Consider all 5 senses as you create a space that really inspires you, where you look forward to stitching every day. Read the suggestions, then write down how you will prepare your space.

SIGHT:

- **Pick a comfy spot** where you can maintain good knitting posture.
- **Create good lighting** – consider purchasing an Ott light or similar daylight lamp.
- **Fill a bowl** with some of your favorite skeins, or a vase with pretty needles.

SOUND:

- **Queue up your favorite knitting podcasts** (we're loving the Grocery Girls right now)
- **Create** a knitting music playlist.
- **Find a new Netflix series** (we're partial to The Crown).
- **Purchase a small fountain** to add the soothing sound of water to your space.

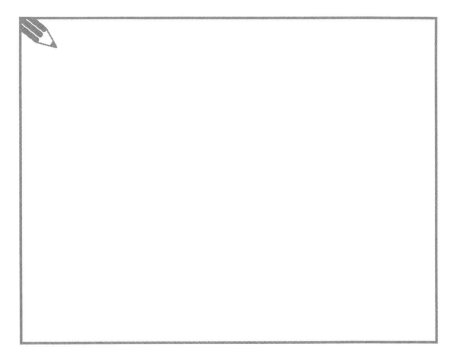

SMELL:

- **Treat yourself to a new candle** (we just found Bath and Bodyworks "Sunlit Cashmere").
- **Get an essential oil diffuser** (try this "Anthro Bomb" blend from Young Living: 2 drops each Geranium, Grapefruit, Orange and Blue Spruce oils).
- **Try placing a lavender sachet** in your knitting bag – each time you open it you will inhale and relax!
- **Rub a drop of essential oil** between your palms and inhale before you knit.

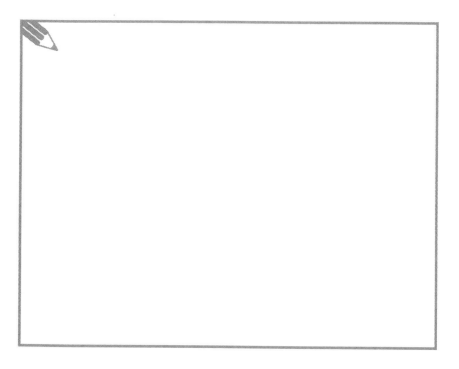

- **Treat yourself to a new tea or coffee** that you save for knitting time.
- **Make a batch of crockpot spiced nuts** to snack on while you knit.
- **You can never go wrong with chocolate.**

FEEL:

- **It's all about the yarn!** Make it delicious!
  (See next section...)

ACTION ITEM:

☐ Share your ideas or a photo of your finished knitting **nest in the LoopsLove Challenge Facebook Group!** http://bit.ly/loops-love

PICK THREE PROJECTS.

This can be three projects already in your stash, three new projects, or a combination. You want three projects so you have the freedom to pick up whichever one you're in the mood for each day.

When choosing, follow these guidelines:

- At least one should be a mindless project you can memorize, and work without referencing the pattern or a chart.
- All 3 projects must be things you are excited about creating – no "obligation" projects, commission work, test knits or old stuff from your WIP pile that you always dread working on!
- Preferably, no deadlines (baby gift, wedding gift etc.)
- Ideally, one project will include a technique that's new to you, but not too difficult.

PROJECT 1

Yarn:

Needles/Hook/Tools:

Pattern:

PROJECT 2

Yarn:

Needles/Hook/Tools:

Pattern:

PROJECT 3

Yarn:

Needles/Hook/Tools:

Pattern:

Now, gather up your supplies and put each project in its own project bag. Stumped? Here are a few of our favorite all-time projects:

Effin Scarf
by Loretta McCullough
FREE HERE:
http://bit.ly/effinscarf

Eyelet Ponchini
by StevenBe
http://bit.ly/eyelet-ponchini

Tea House Wrap
by Alexandra Tavel
(CROCHET)
http://bit.ly/tea-house-wrap

Vinyarnsa
by Shelley Brander
FREE HERE:
http://bit.ly/patterns-knitters

Osage Cowl
by Gina Hills
FREE HERE:
http://bit.ly/patterns-knitters

3-Color Cashmere Cowl
by Joji Locatelli
http://bit.ly/3Color-Cashmere

ACTION ITEM:

☐ Once you've decided, share your project choices in the LoopsLove Challenge Facebook group! http://bit.ly/loops-love

CONSIDER COLOR CAREFULLY.

Color is a very personal thing. For this challenge, be sure your yarn colors make you happy. Also, we suggest using a different color/palette for each of your three projects, so you can choose the one each day that suits your mood.

Project 1 color/s:

Project 2 color/s:

Project 3 color/s:

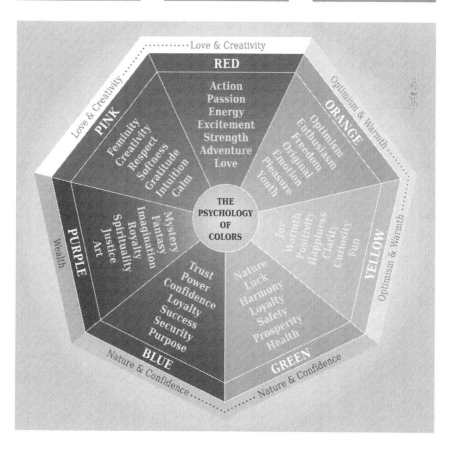

STAY ACCOUNTABLE.

Take these steps to be sure you stay accountable, complete the challenge, and get on your way to establishing a lifelong habit that you love!

☐ DOWNLOAD A HABIT TRACKER ON YOUR PHONE.

We like Today Tracker for iPhone, and Streak Tracker or Loop Habit Tracker for Android.

Today Habit tracker Streaks   Loop Habit Tracker

Don't have a smartphone? Do it the old fashioned way by crossing off each day, below:

1	2	3	4	5	6	7	8	9	10	11
12	13	14	15	16	17	18	19	20	21	

☐ Post your progress in the LoopsLove Challenge Facebook group.
http://bit.ly/loops-love

☐ Find an accountability buddy – in the Facebook group or in the 21-Day
Challenge Thread of the Loopalicious Ravelry group.

☐ Share your challenges, too! If you miss a day or fall behind, don't be
afraid to share.

☐ If you fall behind, don't beat yourself up. Life happens...just pick it back
up and go!

SHARE THE LOVE.

☐ KNIT IN PUBLIC!

Pick a public place (like a park, library, coffee shop...) and make it a point to knit there. When people ask you about it, be ready with resources – a local yarn store or online source to help them get started ☺

☐ SHARE YOUR PROGRESS ON YOUR OWN SOCIAL MEDIA.

Use #loopslovechallenge and be sure to mention @loops (Facebook) and @loopslove (Instagram) so we can see your posts!

CHAPTER 2:

The 90-Day LoopsLove Stash Challenge

INTRO:

Overcoming Stash Guilt.

We all have it.

And we should all let go of it!

A stash is simply part of being a knitter or crocheter. And the sooner you start to shift away from thinking of it as "stash" or "leftovers," and shift toward thinking of it as a "collection," the happier you will be :)

Our hope in creating this workbook, and the accompanying Challenge group on Facebook, is that you will learn to love your collection, and re-visit it again and again.

After all, our collections are great reminders of our knitting journey – where we've come from, what we've learned. And when you pair them with a perfect pattern (and perhaps a new skein or two), you can experience a wonderful melding together of past, present and future!

And one more thing: **The 90-Day Challenge timeframe** is just a suggestion. We've found this to be an optimal timeframe to keep you on-track without getting overwhelmed. But if you want to Marie Kondo it in a weekend, or do a little each month for a year, that's fine too! It's your stash...you're in control!

BUILD YOUR PROJECT USING OUR P+P+P+P FORMULA.

Over the years at Loops, we've found there's a simple formula for learning to love your stash. It's P+P+P+P: Purge, Pretty, Pick, and Pair.

☐ PURGE:

Your first move is to gather all of your stash in one place (go ahead, pull out those under-bed containers ;-) organize it, purge it and make it pretty. Be aggressive with the purging. Use the "Kon-Mari" - method: Hold each skein in your hand, and if it doesn't bring you joy, it needs to go. Consider donating to a local women's shelter or cancer hospital, or selling it on Ravelry.com or in a garage sale.

☐ PRETTY:

Now, take the joyful skeins that remain, and organize them. There are three primary ways to do this.

1. By color	2. By gauge
	3. By project

If you make a lot of garments, you might want to organize by project. Put each grouping of yarn, along with the pattern, into a clear bag or storage container, and line them up in your stash space.

If you make a wide variety of projects in all different gauges, you might want to store fingering with fingering, worsted with worsted, and so on.

If you make mostly accessories, I suggest organizing by color. This is my personal preference.

GET CREATIVE WITH STORAGE AND DISPLAY IDEAS!

- Wooden crates attached with zip ties
- Pegboard and hooks or dowel rods
- Antique cabinets and chests

- Hanging shoe bags
- Wine racks
- Glass vases, antique canisters, and baskets for special skeins

HERE ARE SOME ORGANIZATIONAL PHOTOS FROM STASH CHALLENGE GRADUATES TO INSPIRE YOU:

Danielle's cubbies

Diane's circle of yarn

Janet's yarn armoire

Gayle's shoes bags

Maryann's combo yarn/kids room

Loretta's cabinet

☐ PICK.

Now, let's get you really excited about working from your collection! Once you've organized everything, chances are you've re-discovered a skein or two you REALLY love. Narrow it down, then write in the box your very favorite skein, including the brand/dyer, color name, yardage and gauge (number of recommended stitches per inch – from the yarn label):

STASH YARN FOR PROJECT #1.

STASH YARN FOR PROJECT #2.

☐ PAIR.

Next, let's create two projects: An easier, more mindless project and a more challenging one. The good news is, you don't have to be limited to JUST your stash skeins. You can add some new ones! Often, adding something new is just what you need to get you really excited to use stash yarn. Let's start with some of the Loops Troops' favorite de-stashing projects:

Fake a Fade Cowl

by Shelley Brander

http://bit.ly/patterns-knitters

Honeybead Cowl

by Gina Hills

http://bit.ly/patterns-knitters

Lulu Cowl

by Shelley Brander

http://bit.ly/patterns-knitters

Marled Magic Mystery Shawl

by Stephen West

http://bit.ly/marled-magic

Stashbuster Shawl

by UrbanGypsyZ Designs

http://bit.ly/stash-buster

Stash-o-motastic Mitts

by Donna Herron

http://bit.ly/stash-motastic

ZickZack Scarf

by Christy Kamm

http://bit.ly/zickzack-scarf

Guiltbuster Scarf

by Shelley Brander

http://bit.ly/patterns-knitters

MY STASH-BUSTING PROJECTS WILL BE:

I need to add the following yarn/s to the project
(fill in gauge, yardage amounts, and any color desires):

Now it may be time to go shopping! A new skein or two can really get you excited about your project. So head to your local yarn store, back to your collection, or to LoopsLove.com to choose your additional yarns.

Write the new skein info in here (brand, yarn name, color, gauge, yardage):

Need some help building your perfect project?

Email a photo of your favorite skein from your collection,

plus requests/notes/pattern desires,

to support@loopslove.com

SET UP ACCOUNTABILITY.

Challenges are more fun with friends! Take these steps to make sure you stay accountable and finish your project.

☐ **DOWNLOAD A HABIT TRACKER ON YOUR PHONE**
(see suggestions in Chapter 1). Don't have a smartphone? Do it the old fashioned way by crossing off each day, below:

1	2	3	4	5	6	7	8	9	10	11
12	13	14	15	16	17	18	19	20	21	

☐ Post your progress in the LoopsLove Stash Challenge Group on Facebook. http://bit.ly/loops-love

☐ Find an accountability buddy in the Facebook group – agree to message each other regularly and share your progress.

☐ Share your challenges, too! If you miss a day or fall behind, don't be afraid to share.

☐ If you fall behind, don't beat yourself up. Life happens...just pick it back up and go!

☐ SHARE YOUR PROGRESS ON YOUR OWN SOCIAL MEDIA.

Use #loopslovechallenge and be sure to mention @loops (Facebook) and @loopsyarn (Instagram) so we can see your posts!

When you've completed the challenge, it's time to celebrate! Treat yourself to a new project, a bubble bath, or even a glass of champagne! Write how you plan to celebrate below...then treat yourself!

CHAPTER 3

The WIP-It Challenge

WIPs. Works In Progress.

Sometimes also known as U.F.O.s (UnFinished Objects).

We all have them.

Even the most dedicated and linear knitters among us. And that's perfectly okay...

Unless they are a source of guilt.

As you work through this guide, we'll outline a proven strategy that can help you WIP IT -- whip your stash guilt - for good.

Along the way, we'll have a lot of fun together.

SO TO PARAPHRASE THE IMMORTAL WORDS OF DEVO...

"When a project comes along,
you must WIP it.
On your needles for too long?
You must WIP it.
When something's going wrong
You must WIP it.
Now WIP it.
Into shape.
Pick it up...
On straights.
Go for it.
Move ahead.
Don't you detest it...
It's not to late
To WIP it.
WIP it good!"

LET'S WIP IT, TOGETHER!

☐ PULL OUT ALL THOSE WIPS.

This is the hardest part. But it can be quick and relatively painless. All you need is a little resolve – and the support of your fellow Challenge members!

Go digging – in your stash, in the closet, under the bed…

And if you're like us, you'll need to empty out all those knitting bags!

Pull out any Works In Progress and put them all in one place where you can easily sort through them (a dining room table works great).

Pause and take a moment to congratulate yourself for facing all of your WIPs.

Now is a great time to take a "before" photo of all your WIPs. Then move on to Step 2.

ACTION ITEM:

☐ Post a photo of all your WIPs in the LoopsLove 90-Day Challenge group. http://bit.ly/loops-love

☐ IDENTIFY, RE-BAG AND PRIORITIZE.

Now we're getting down to the knitty gritty (pun intended).

FIRST, **you may need to do a bit of detective work.**

Often, our WIPs can get separated from the pattern, or even from their needles (parked on waste yarn or on interchangeable cords). Yarn labels can also get misplaced. So, for each WIP in your stash, print and complete a WIP ID tag (we've included a handy link to a printable sheet - see next page). Be sure to assign a target completion date for each project.

WIP ID TAG

Project name: ....

Designer: ....

Needle size/s: ....

Yarn brand/s: ....

Yarn color/s: ....

Do I have enough yarn to complete the project? .... Yes .... No

Do I need more needles? .... Yes ....No

Do I need any other notions or tools? ....
....

Target completion date: ....

Notes: ....
....
....

☐ DOWNLOAD THE PRINTABLE WIP
ID TAG SHEET

http://bit.ly/wipidtags

SECOND, you may need to re-organize your WIPs.

Consider purchasing large, clear ziplock bags and placing each project in a like-size bag, with your WIP ID tag visible. Hint: Search "Ziplock Big Bags" on Amazon for several choices of sizes.

THIRD, prioritize your WIPs according to project completion date.

Place your #1 priority project in a pretty project bag, and commit to taking any steps needed to complete it (see Step 4).

*Angela's WIPs
Before*

*Angela's WIPs
After*

☐ THE SORBET PROJECT KNIT-ALONG.

After you've organized your WIPs is a great time to cast on a "sorbet project." This is a super-simple project that "cleanses the palate" – giving you a little break before you dive back into a bigger project.

We've included one of our favorites, the "Malacowl." It's a super-simple feather-and-fan pattern that knits up quickly with a single skein of Malabrigo Rios or other worsted weight yarn (this is also a great stash-busting project!).

Check out the LoopsLove Challenge Facebook group (http://bit.ly/loops-love) for previous examples of others' beautiful Malacowls to inspire you. Then go ahead, cast one on – and you'll be binding off in no time!

ACTION ITEM:

> What yarn will you be using for your MalaCowl? Go the LoopsLove Challenge Group and post a photo of the yarn you've chosen. http://bit.ly/loops-love

MalaCowl

A LOOPS ORIGINAL

YARN:	TOOLS:	GAUGE:
Malabrigo Rios, 1 skein	#10 16" or 24" circulars	Approx. 4 sts/inch

DIRECTIONS:

Cast on 96 stitches. Join in the round, being careful not to twist.

Row 1: K2tog 4 times, *(kfb 8 times, k2tog 8 times)*, repeat from * to * to last 8 sts, k2tog 4 times.

Rows 2, 3 and 4: Knit all sts.

Repeat rows 1 through 4 to desired length. Bind off loosely.

Note: To make a cowl that is wider and not as tall, cast on 120 sts and follow the pattern as written. Either way, it just takes one skein!

☐ BACK TO THE WIPS: GETTING UN-STUCK.

Alright, you're ready to dive back in to your WIP process. The next step is to go to your organized WIP project bags and take them out, one by one. Ask yourself: Why did I stop working on this? Did I get bored? Did I get distracted with a shiny new project? Or did I get stuck?

THERE ARE SEVERAL WAYS YOU MIGHT HAVE GOTTEN STUCK:

1.   You made a mistake and you weren't sure how to fix it
2.   You encountered a technique or abbreviation you weren't familiar with
3.   You put down the project and forgot where you were in the pattern

If you got stuck, now is the time to get un-stuck. Take the steps needed to get the project back on track – and then WRITE DOWN the answer/fix when you find it. You can write this on the notes section of the project's WIP ID tag.

HERE ARE STRATEGIES FOR EACH OF THE STICKING POINTS:

1.   You made a mistake and you weren't sure how to fix it
     The fix: Go to your local yarn store or email photos to support@loopslove.com **for help.**

2.   You encountered a technique or abbreviation you weren't familiar with
     The fix: Search Google or Youtube for the info you need, or email support@loopslove.com

3.   You put down the project and forgot where you were in the pattern
     The fix: You know your own knitting the best...so set aside time to refamiliarize yourself with the pattern, then mark on the pattern where you are. (It's ok to mark on the pattern – the knitting police will not come to your house!)

☐ TO FROG OR NOT TO FROG?

Sometimes, the best decision is simply to frog the project ("Rip-it, rip-it!"). This decision can be hard, but not as hard as leaving the yarn to languish and "die" in your stash!

HERE ARE REASONS YOU MIGHT CHOOSE TO FROG:

- You got bored with it and can't stand to look at the pattern anymore.
- It turns out the pattern is way above your skill level and you don't really have the desire to learn the technique.
- It turns out the yarn was not the right fit for the pattern (e.g. mohair for a pattern you keep having to tink back on...too frustrating).
- While you were knitting, you had that sinking feeling that the pattern was really not your style, you would never wear/use it, your gauge was way off, etc.
- You lost the pattern and can't remember what it was.

If any of these situations exist, it's better to give the yarn a chance at a new life! This is your permission...go ahead and gently unravel the project, hand-winding it into a ball as you go.

Pro tip: You can also take the extra step of re-winding the skeins with a swift and winder (either at your local yarn store or on your own set at home). Having the yarn neatly re-caked will give you extra inspiration to cast on with a new project. FRESH START. Yay!

ACTION STEP:

☐ Post a photo of your freshly frogged and re-caked yarn in Facebook LoopsLove Challenge group. http://bit.ly/loops-love
If you need pattern inspiration for your frogged yarn, ask your fellow Challengers, or email support@loopslove.com

STEP 6:

☐ PREVENTION

Commit to make a WIP ID tag for all of your future projects. Make a tag, with yarn, needle and pattern info, before you even cast on – and you will never have another Unidentified Unfinished Project!

It's also a great idea to keep a knitting journal. You can copy your ID tag info into the journal as you add new projects. This has the added benefit of logging your whole knitting journey, so you can always look back and see how far you've come!

STEP 7:

☐ CAST BACK ON...AND SHARE!

Congratulations!

All of your WIPs are organized and tagged!
You've completed your sorbet project!
And you're ready to cast back on – and complete – your favorite WIP.

GREAT JOB!

ACTION STEP:

☐ Share a photo of your favorite WIP – either back in progress, or completed – in the LoopsLove Challenge Group.
http://bit.ly/loops-love

Remember to cheer on your fellow Challengers to the finish line.

Now you're ready for the next Challenge...Love to Give!

CHAPTER 4

The Love to Give Challenge

Why We Love to Give.

What's the one gift that will never be re-gifted or thrown away?

A handstitched one, of course!

As knitters and crocheters, we all know the power of a beautiful handmade gift. We all look forward to that moment when someone we love unwraps the present that we've poured our heart, soul and precious hours into making.

But sometimes we tend to bite off more than we can chew, especially as the holidays approach.

The secrets to avoiding holiday overwhelm? The right planning, the right patterns, and the right support from your favorite community :)

This workbook will help you get started right now. We've included our favorite strategies and some of our all-time favorite gift patterns.

So let's jump in together, and challenge each other to give more love this holiday season!

☐ COMPLETE THE LOVE TO GIVE FRAMEWORK

Gift knitting isn't about working harder. It's about working smarter!

Use this template to do an honest calculation of your stitching time between now and Christmas, then figure out how many projects you can reasonably make.

Line 1:

I can comfortably commit to an average of .... hours of stitching/week

Line 2:

I have .... weeks left between now and Christmas (or other big date)

Line 3:

Multiple Line 1 X Line 2 = ...This is your total stitching time budget!

Line 4:

On average, I will commit ....hours to making each gift

Line 5:

Divide your answer in Line 3 by your answer in Line 4 = ...

This is the total number of projects you can comfortably make in your timeframe.

STEP 2:

☐ DECIDE ON YOUR GIFT PATTERNS.

When it comes to gift knitting and crocheting, you want to choose your patterns wisely. Over the years at Loops, we've identified some strategies that tend to make for BIG gift stitching success!

- **GO EASY**
  Choose easier patterns that you can work on in any situation – watching TV, in the car, on the go. You'll be more likely to complete them.

- **THINK SMALL**
  A baby hat can be just as cherished as a blanket. A chunky scarf may actually get more wear than a fingering weight sweater. Lean toward fast, fun-to-knit accessories.

- **BUY BIG**
  Choose thicker weights (DK, worsted, chunky, bulky) and size up on your needles for faster results.

- **WASH, RINSE, REPEAT**
  Patterns are like recipes. When you find one you love, don't be afraid to make it again! You'll get faster and faster each time you make it. Choose a pattern that can work for LOTS of your recipients, and just vary the color for each person, to keep from getting bored.

STEP 3:

☐ GIFTABLE PATTERNS.

To save you a bunch of searching, we've included 12 original Loops patterns at the end of this chapter! All of these are time-tested favorites for gift knitting and crocheting. **The patterns include:**

- Christmas Creep
- Double Seed Cowl
- Effin Scarf
- Fibonacci Blanket
- Gin and Juice
- Hookin Scarf
- La Novela
- Lazy Girl Hat
- Lulu Cashmere Cowl
- Shoji Cowl
- Snooty Cape
- Sooner Pompom Hat

You'll also find a bunch of free patterns that are great for gifting on the Free Patterns tab of LoopsLove.com: http://bit.ly/patterns-knitters

Some of our favorite giftable patterns from our Free Patterns tab on LoopsLove.com include:

- Cantaloop
- Osage Cowl
- Melanie's Shawl
- Three-Way Wrap
- Knotty But Nice
- Mitzi's Easy Rib Cowl
- Necks Big Thing
- Suede Fringe Scarf

☐ COMPLETE YOUR GIFT STITCH TO-DO LIST.

We've all been there. The countdown to Christmas begins, and just when you think you have all your gifts planned – OOPS – you forgot the 1st grade teacher! So we created this handy worksheet that you can use to plan and prioritize all of your gift stitching.

Obviously, you've gotta prioritize :) Set realistic goals and don't feel like you have to make for everyone.

The surprise: Personally, I like to surprise someone each year who wouldn't possibly be expecting a handmade gift – but who has made a real difference in my life, even if it's in a seemingly small way. Maybe it's the UPS guy (we LOVE Freddie, our UPS hero at Loops!), or the funny barista who makes your latte each day.

And one other piece of advice: Only knit or crochet for those who will appreciate the effort. If you never see your niece wearing what you've made, she may not be "knitworthy." It's ok to just get her an iTunes gift card, and move on to others who will love and appreciate your efforts.

MY GIFT STITCH TO-DO LIST
HOLIDAY .... (YEAR)

RECIPIENT	PROJECT	YARN	NEEDLES	PRIORITY	DONE!
Spouse/S.O.					
Mom					
Dad					
Son					
Grandkid					
Brother					
Sister					
Bestie					
New Mom-to-be					
Teacher/Coach					
Stitching buddy					
Total Surprise Recipient					

ACTION ITEM:

☐ Post a photo of your completed Gift Stitch To-Do List in the LoopsLove Challenge Facebook group http://bit.ly/loops-love

☐ JOIN THE GIFT-ALONG!

Let's do a great gift project together! Lots of people in the Facebook group have made Gin and Juice (see end of this chapter). For Gin and Juice you'll need 109 yards of bulky yarn and about the same amount of a finer yarn.

Some yarn suggestions...

BULKY:

- **Forget-Me-Not**
  http://bit.ly/plymouthyarn

- **Rasta**
  http://bit.ly/malabrigo-rasta

- **Manos Franca**
  http://bit.ly/manosfranca

FINE:

- **Freia Merino/Silk Ombre Fingering**
  http://bit.ly/freiamerino

- **Hedgehog Fibres Sock**
  http://bit.ly/hedgehogsock

- **Llama Lace Melange**
  http://bit.ly/llamalace

- **Manos Alegria**
  http://bit.ly/manos212

Ideally, you want the yarns to have good contrast – in color, fiber or both. It's fun to use a long color-changing repeat yarn for either the bulky or the finer yarn, but it's not critical. And a good wet-blocking can really transform the look and size of this piece, so don't be afraid to soak it!

ACTION ITEM:

☐ What yarn will you use for your Gin and Juice, and who are you making it for? Go to the Facebook group and post a photo of the yarn you've chosen or the person you're knitting it for! http://bit.ly/loops-love

☐ TAG IT!

Go ahead and make a gift tag for each project as you complete it. You can even wrap each gift and tag it, so everything is ready to go under the tree as soon as the holidays arrive!

Handmade just for you with Loops Love!

To: _____

From: _____

Fiber content: _____

Pattern name: _____

Care instructions: _____

Handmade just for you with Loops Love!

To: _____

From: _____

Fiber content: _____

Pattern name: _____

Care instructions: _____

Handmade just for you with Loops Love!

To: _____

From: _____

Fiber content: _____

Pattern name: _____

Care instructions: _____

Handmade just for you with Loops Love!

To: _____

From: _____

Fiber content: _____

Pattern name: _____

Care instructions: _____

☐ DOWNLOAD THE PRINTABLE ID TAG

http://bit.ly/handmade-tags

STEP 7:

☐ YARN-Y WRAPPING INSPO

Here's a great way to use up those scraps or those sparkly or funky-colored skeins you probably won't ever knit or crochet with. Keep your leftovers with your wrapping paper and whip up these ideas to adorn your packages!

Remember, it doesn't have to be fancy or expensive to be adorable!

Christmas Creep

BY THE LOOPS TROOPS

YARN:	TOOLS:	GAUGE:
83-100 yards superbulky yarn	#19 needles, straight or circular	Approx. 1.5 its = 1"

DIRECTIONS:

Cast on 12 stitches.

K1, *YO, k2tog* repeat from * to * to last stitch, K1

Repeat this row for entire scarf.

Bind off.

Seam ends into cowl if desired.

Enjoy!

Double Seed Cowl

BY SHELLEY BRANDER

YARN:	TOOLS:	GAUGE:
300 yards chunky yarns	#13 circular needles 32-40" long, stitch marker	Approx. 3 sts = 1"

DIRECTIONS:

Cast on 132 stitches.

Join into round and place marker, being careful not to twist.

K2, P2 for 2 rounds
P2, K2 for 2 rounds

Repeat last 4 rounds until 5-6 yards of yarn remain.
Bind off loosely.

To make tri-color version shown at right:
Work 4" of each color, then change colors and continue pattern as written.
You'll need 100 yds x 3 colors.

Effin Scarf

BY LORETTA MCCOLLOUGH

YARN:	TOOLS:	GAUGE:
250-300 yards any fingering, sport, DK or worsted yarn with drape	US #13, plus possibly a #15-#17 needle for casting on and binding off	Approx. 2 sts/inch - not critical to the success of the scarf

Loretta developed this seemingly simple scarf for nearly five years! We all kept bugging her for the pattern and she replied, "Oh that effin' scarf..." But she finally wrote it up!

Join into round and place marker, being careful not to twist.

With #13 needles, cast on 70 stitches VERY LOOSELY. If you can't be VERY LOOSE, use a #15 or #17 needle to cast on, then switch to the #13 needles for the body of the scarf.

Knit 3 rows.
Next row: K2, YO, K1, YO, K1, YO, knit to end.
Repeat the last row until you have approximately 180 stitches on your needle, or you are nearly out of yarn. Bind off all stitches VERY LOOSELY, or use a #15 or #17 needle to bind off.

Fibonacci Blanket

BY THE LOOPS TROOPS

YARN:	TOOLS:	GAUGE:
Chunky wool or blend, 2 skeins warm colors and 2 cool. 150 yds ea.	US #10.5, 24-inch circular needles	3.5 sts = 1 inch

Note: 2 rows equals one stripe.

Cast on 88 stitches.

Knit 3 stripes (6 rows) in Color A.

Knit 5 stripes (10 rows) in Color B.

Knit 8 stripes (16 rows) in Color C.

Next, start with Color D continue knitting all stitches, repeating stripe number sequence (3, 5, 8) as you continue to work through the color sequence (i.e. 3 stripes D, 5 stripes A, 8 stripes B, 3 stripes C, 5 stripes D etc.) until you are almost out of yarn, then bind off loosely.

FINISHING

If desired, crochet a border around blanket in any of the four colors.

Gin and Juice

BY SHELLEY BRANDER

YARN:	TOOLS:	GAUGE:
1 skein Bulky (109 yds) and 1 skein laceweight or fingering (109 yds)	#13 straight or circular US needles, tapestry needle	2 sts = 1" (not critical)

DIRECTIONS:

With #13 needles and your preferred cast-on method, cast on 30 sts with bulky yarn.

**Knit one row in bulky.
Purl one row in bulky.
Switch to laceweight and knit one row.
Still with laceweight, purl one row.**

Repeat from ** until you have about 3 yards of bulky remaining, ending with a laceweight purl row.

Using bulky, cast off loosely in knit stitch.
Soak your cowl in warm water and pin out on blocking mat, opening up the lace stitches. Once it dries, thread the tail of the bulky yarn (from the cast-off) onto a tapestry needle, and use mattress stitch to seam the cast-on edge of your cowl to the bind-off edge. Weave in ends.

Hookin Scarf

BY SHERRI TORREZ

YARN:	TOOLS:	GAUGE:
200 yards any smooth DK or light worsted yarn, or smooth ribbon yarn	Size L (8mm), or N (9mm) if you are a tight crocheter, 2 locking stitch markers	7 st = 4"

DESIGNER NOTES:

Please do not skip the stitch markers. That last loop can be tricky to pick up. Gauge is not critical, but you want your stitches very loose.

DIRECTIONS:

Chain 51.
Row 1: 1 sc in the 2nd ch from the hook and in each ch to the end. Ch 3, turn.

Row 2: 2 sc in the 2nd ch from the hook. Place marker in the 1st sc made.
1 sc in the next ch, 1 sc in each sc to the end.
Ch 3, turn.

Repeat Row 2 until you run out of yarn (approx. 26 rows).

Cut yarn and weave in ends.

La Novela

BY SHERRI TORREZ, LOOPS

YARN:	TOOLS:	GAUGE:
330 yards luxury merino-blend fingering or sport weight yarn	G-6 4.00mm Crochet Hook	5 Vsts = 4" after blocking

ABBREVIATIONS:

Ch = Chain

Sc = Single Crochet

Dc = Double Crochet

Sk = Skip

St = Stitch

Sl st = Slip Stitch

Vst = V-Stitch (dc, ch 3, dc) in same stitch or space

DESIGNER'S NOTE:

As you follow the pattern, you make a Picot Stitch (Ch 4, 1 Sc in 3rd Ch from hook, Ch 1) at the beginning and end of each row, creating a lacy edge-as-you-go effect.

DIRECTIONS: CH 4.

Row 1: 4 Dc in 4th Ch from hook. Ch 4, turn.

Row 2: 1 Sc in 3rd Ch from hook, Ch 1. Work 1 Vst in 1st Dc.

Sk 3 Dc, work 1 Dc in top of Ch3, Ch 6, sl st in same Ch where Dc was just made, Ch 4, turn. 1 Sc in 3rd Ch from hook, Ch 1. Sl st in 3rd Ch of Ch6.

Row 3: Ch 4, 1 Sc in 3rd Ch from hook, Ch 1. Vst in same Ch where Sl st was just made. Sk 3 Chs and 1 Dc, Vst in space between Vsts of previous row. (Not in the center of the Vst.) Sk 1 Dc and 3 Chs, Dc in last Dc, Ch 6, Sl st in last Dc, Ch 4, turn. 1 Sc in 3rd Ch from hook, Ch 1. Sl st in 3rd Ch of Ch6.

Row 4: Ch 4, 1 Sc in 3rd Ch from hook, Ch 1. Vst in same Ch where Sl st was just made. *Sk 3 Chs and 1 Dc, Vst in space between Vsts of previous row. (Not in the center of the Vst.)*
Repeat * 1 more time. Sk 1 Dc and 3 Chs, Dc in last Dc, Ch 6, Sl st in last Dc, Ch 4, turn. 1 Sc in 3rd Ch from hook, Ch 1. Sl st in 3rd Ch of Ch6.

Rows 5-47 (or until you run out of yarn): Repeat Row 4, but repeat * 1 additional time each row. (i.e. Row 5: Repeat * 2 more times, Row 6: Repeat * 3 more times, etc.)

Cut yarn and weave in ends. Blocking is recommended, with an emphasis on length.

Lazy Girl Hat

BY TRACY KEETER

YARN:	TOOLS:	GAUGE:
1 skein Adriafil KnitCol (137 yards) plus 20 yards contrast DK or worsted	#5 and #6 16" circulars plus #6 DPNs (or magic loop)	5.5 sts = 1" in stockinette

BRIM:

With #5 16" circular needles (or 32-40" circs if doing magic loop), cast on 120 stitches with brim color (any DK or worsted yarn with some "give" will work). Work in 2x2 rib until you get tired of it (about 1-2 inches).

BODY OF HAT:

Change to #6 needles and KnitCol, and knit for 5-6 inches.

Work decrease rounds (switching to DPNs as needed):
k10, k2 tog around
knit 1 round
k9, k2tog around
knit 1 round
k8, k2tog around

From here, decrease every round:
k7, k2tog around
k6, k2tog around
k5, k2tog around
k4, k2tog around
k3, k2tog around
k2, k2 tog around
k1, k2 tog around
k2 tog around.

With tapestry needle, run yarn through remaining stitches and cinch tight. Weave ends.

Lulu Cashmere Cowl

BY SHELLEY BRANDER

YARN:	TOOLS:	GAUGE:
Cashmere worsted weight yarn, 72 yds x 6 colors	#10 straight or circular needles 8 - 3/4" buttons	Approx. 4 sts = 1 inch after blocking Finished size: 28"x14"

Note: Slip the first stitch of every row throughout. Cast on 50 sts in color A (blue/grey).
Knitting every row, knit through the entire skein of color A (approx 36 rows), ending at the end of an even-numbered row. Break yarn.

With color B (lavender) knit 18 rows. Break yarn.

With color C (spots) knit 10 rows. Break yarn.

With color D (teal) knit the full skein (approx. 36 rows). Break yarn.

With C knit 18 rows. Break yarn.

With color E (green multi) knit almost the full skein (approx. 34 rows) then cast off loosely.

With color F (pink) and right side facing, pick up and knit 90 sts along long side of scarf. Knit 16 rows. Break yarn.

With C, knit one row, then cast off loosely.

Return to where you cast off in color E (green multi), and using color B with the right side up, pick up and knit 56 stitches along shorter side of scarf (includes the end of vertical stripe in color F). Knit 2 rows.

Buttonhole row, still in color B): k3 *YO, k2tog, k5* repeat from * to last 4 sts, YO, k2tog, k2.
Knit 3 more rows with color B then bind off loosely.

Weave in ends, steam block, sew on buttons, enjoy!

Shoji Cowl
BY SHERRI TORREZ

YARN:	TOOLS:	GAUGE:
290 yards chunky or bulky yarn (shown in Shalimar Breathless Cush)	Size J hook, tapestry needle	7 dc/ch1 repeats = 4", 5 rows =6"

ABBREVIATIONS:
ch=chain
st=stitch
dc=double crochet
sk=skip

DIRECTIONS: Cowl is worked in rows like a scarf, then seamed together to form a ring. Fringe is attached to only one long edge.

Ch 30
Row 1: 1 dc in 6th ch from hook, *ch1, sk 1 ch, 1 dc in next ch* repeat from * 11 more times, turn (13 spaces).
Row 2: Ch4, sk 1 ch, 1 dc in next dc, *ch1, sk 1 ch, 1 dc in next dc* repeat from * 10 more times, ch 1, sk 1 ch, 1 dc in third ch of beginning ch of previous row, turn (13 spaces).

Rows 3-60: Repeat row 2.
Cut yarn, leaving a 24" tail for sewing.

FINISHING:
Hold just-completed edge of cowl and beginning edge of cowl together to form a ring, being careful not to twist. Thread tail into tapestry needle and sew these ends together, matched up stitch for stitch. Cut tail and weave in ends.

FRINGE: Cut yarn into 16" lengths, 20 bundles of 6 strands each. Using crochet hook, attach bundles of fringe to one long side of cowl, in every 3rd space.

Snooty Cape
BY THE LOOPS TROOPS

YARN:	TOOLS:	GAUGE:
545 yards chunky alpaca	#10, 10.5 and 13 circulars - 24"	3.5 sts = 1 inch on #10 needles

ABBREVIATIONS:

RS: right side

WS: wrong side

CB8: Slip next 4 stitches onto cable needle and, holding yarn and cable needle in back of work, K4, then knit the 4 stitches from cable needle

CF8: Same as CB8, except hold cable needle and yarn in front of work

DIRECTIONS:

Loosely cast on 56 sts. (Optional: Do a provisional cast on. This gives you the option of doing a three needle bind off or kitchener stitch to finish).

Row 1(RS): K3, P2, K8, P2, K2, P2, K8, P2, K8, P2, K2, P2, K8, P2, K3

Row 2 and all WS rows: Knit the knits and purl the purls (P3, K2, P8, K2, P2, K2, P8, K2, P2, K2, P8, K2, P3)

Rows (RS) 3, 5: same as set up row

Row 7 (cable row): K3, P2, CB8, P2, K2, P2, CB8, P2, CF8, P2, K2, P2, CF8, P2, K3

Row 8: same as other wrong side rows

Repeat rows 1-8 being careful to always "turn" your cables on the right side. Work for 40" or until piece fits snugly around shoulders. Cast off, loosely, in preferred method and/or sew ends together or graft ends

With size 10.5 needle pick up 108 sts (approximately 3 for every 5 sts), join and work 2" in 2 x 2 rib, At this time, change to size 10 needles and continue in pattern until desired depth of cowl or until just enough yarn is left to bind off loosely. Voila! You are done.

Wear it proudly, but not too snootily!

Sooner Pompom Hat

BY LORETTA MCCOLLOUGH

YARN:	TOOLS:	GAUGE:
Rowan Wool Cotton (50% Merino, 50% Cotton) 113m, 1 ball each color	#3 (16" circular or DPNs), #6 (16" circ or DPNs), and #6 DPNS	5.5 sts/inch

DIRECTIONS

Note: Feel free to experiment with striping, but keep the amount of yarn used relatively even for your two colors. This hat fits an average adult head.

With color A, cast on 112 sts using #3 needles. Join to work in the round and work K2, P2 rib for 10 rows.

Continuing with color A, change to #6 needles and work 2 rows SS (knit every row in the round).

Change to color B and work stripe pattern as follows:
Using color B, work 8 rows.
Using color A, work 8 rows.
Using color B, work 8 rows.
Using color A, work 8 rows.

Keeping stripes in 8-row pattern, begin shaping hat:
Row 1: (K2tog, K6) 14 times, 98 sts. Knit 3 rows.
Row 5: (K2tog, K5) 14 times, 84 sts. Knit 3 rows.
Row 9: (K2tog, K4) 14 times, 70 sts. Knit 3 rows.
Row 13: (K2tog, K3) 14 times, 56 sts. Knit 1 row.
Row 15: (K3tog, K1) 14 times, 28 sts. Knit 1 row.

Cut yarn and thread through remaining 28 sts. Pull up tight and fasten off.

Make 3" pompom using both yarns, and attach to hat.

CHAPTER 5:

The Love Sweaters Challenge

The very first thing I ever knit was a sweater.

I didn't even know you could make a scarf, or a dishcloth, or something else reasonable.

I made a cable sweater – because I wanted to, dang it! And because I was fascinated with the idea of making my own clothing, developing my own knit fabric, and customizing it to my own body in a color and fiber I adore.

Oh and also, because I wanted to show off. Just a little.

I wanted people to ooh and aah over my sweater and then I would casually say, "Oh, this old thing? Yeah, I knit it."

But after 14 years working in yarn, I know there's also a lot of fear surrounding this subject.

Sweaters seem like such a commitment. The cost of the yarn and, more importantly, the time. There's fear and mystery surrounding fit, ease, reading and understanding the pattern, yarn choice, needle size, gauge, and those quirky little schematics.

But take heart. Because we're about to drop our favorite tips, shortcuts and time savers to give you the safety you need to SWEATER LIKE A BOSS. And love the results.

Ready to dive in?

Let's go!

PART 1:

☐ IDENTIFY WHERE YOU ARE ON THE LOOPSLOVE SUCCESS PATH.

Let's check in with that Success Path again. Have you progressed since the last challenge? Where are you now?

Take a moment to consider where you are, because we're going to help you customize your Love Sweaters experience to where you are on your personal stitching journey.

"HAVE YOU PROGRESSED?"

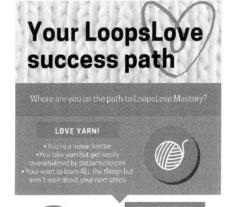

Your LoopsLove success path

Where are you on the path to LoopsLove Mastery?

LOVE YARN!
• You're a newer knitter
• You love yarn but get easily overwhelmed by pattern choices
• Your want to learn ALL the things but aren't sure about your next steps

LOVE TO LEARN
• You love to cast on but often get stuck
• You're starting to amass stash/WIPs
• You're progressing, but still often run into skills you wish you knew
• Certain skills keep you from starting patterns you really love

LOVE SWEATERS
• You've made at least one garment
• You'd like to improve your fit and finishing skills
• You still avoid some patterns because they seem too advanced

LOVE TO DESIGN
• You rarely, if ever, follow the pattern exactly
• You like to take risks with color
• You'd like to expand your design skills

LOVE YOURSELF!
• You see yourself as a fiber artist
• You love sharing photos of yourself in your creations
• You love teaching others
• You can proudly say you're a expert knitter!

ACTION ITEM:

☐ If you haven't already, watch through the Success Path videos in the LoopsLove Challenge Facebook group. Which stage of the LoopsLove Success Path are you in right now? Post and let us know in the private group.

LOOPSLOVE.COM

PART 2

☐ DECIDE ON YOUR SWEATER PATTERN.

We've all had that moment where we fall in love with a photo of a sweater on Ravelry and we're like, "I MUST MAKE THIS."

But a sweater – any sweater, but especially your first sweater – is a commitment. So you want to take your time deciding. Here are some considerations to work through as you decide.

1. CONSIDER YOUR SWEATER TYPE.

There are four basic sweater types, each with their own unique advantages. And let me take a moment to bust a myth: Every type of sweater CAN look good on every body. Often, we hear people say "I can't wear a drop shoulder, it makes me look too boxy." But if you choose the right size, and choose a yarn with the right amount of structure vs. drape, it can be super flattering. So stay open minded here.

The four basic sweater types, in (very) generalized order from simplest to more advanced, are:

• **DROP SHOULDER:**
Made with straight lines everywhere; typically looks best with a yarn that has some drape, and with significant positive ease.

• **RAGLAN:**
Sleeve and body have the same number of rows in the raglan shaping section; can be worked in pieces, bottom up, or top down.

• **YOKE:**
Worked in a single piece; shaping is spread evenly around the circle of the yoke. Colorwork yoke styles are hugely popular right now. They tend to fall straight from the yoke to the hem with minimal waist shaping.

- SET-IN SLEEVE:

The most precise fit; worked in pieces, then seamed.

2. UNDERSTAND SIZE AND EASE.

You're looking at that amazing Ravelry photo and wondering, "What size did they make? Which size should I make? What the heck is 'ease' and how does it affect my size choice?"

Part of the challenge is that most often, designers only include a bust size. And yeah, of course you want the sweater to fit around "the girls." But what matters even more – especially with the current trend of boxier, flow-ier sweaters – is your shoulders and arms.

Nothing is more annoying than a cardigan that's always slipping off your shoulders. And if you're blessed with a bountiful bust but have narrow shoulders, and choose your sweater size based on the bust, you're going to end up with a sweater that swallows you up.

So how do you deal with this dilemma?

First of all, know your most important measurement – the width from the outside of one shoulder to the other. Look for sweater designs that include schematics, and base your size choice on the shoulder width, first and foremost. Choosing boxier sweaters, drop-shoulder styles, and cardigans helps hedge your bets. And if you're after a fitted look, consider Amy Herzog's CustomFit patterns (more info later in this chapter).

To get the same look as that fabulous Ravelry photo, you want to consider how much ease the designer intended, for the sweater to look that way.

Boxy - *by Joji Locatelli*

For the uninitiated, a sweater with "positive ease" has more inches around than your body does. Think of it as "wiggle room" or, more intentionally, "drape room." A sweater can also be designed with "negative ease," meaning if you lay the sweater flat, it has fewer inches around that your body does – and when you wear it, it's intended to stretch to fit your body.

Often, a designer will include a note about how much negative or positive ease they intended between the sweater and the wearer. But if they don't, it's easy to figure out. You just subtract the "Size" from its corresponding "Finished Measurements."

Take for example, the famous "Boxy" sweater by Joji Locatelli. The first size is listed as a 28/30 and the body circumference is 64" – so this sweater in this size is intended to have 34-36" of extra ease. That's a LOT – but if you look at all of the photos, you'll see why.

This design has an exaggerated drop-shoulder, so the extra 17-18" on each side create the fabric that covers your arms, all the way down to the elbow.

Which brings us to our next tip...

3. DIG DEEPER INTO THAT RAVELRY PATTERN PAGE.

A well-vetted Ravelry pattern page offers a ton of "clues" as to whether

this is the sweater for you – so you must dig deeper than that first pretty, shiny photo.

Before you commit to your sweater pattern, look for these 4 things:

- **How many projects?** Choose a pattern that lots of people have already made. Resist being a guinea pig. ☺

- **Read the designer's notes.** For example, Joji explains in the notes that the biggest difference among the sizes of Boxy is the sleeve circumference.

- **Read the comments.** Those who have gone before you can offer lots of insight.

- **Click on the project tab at the top of the page, and scroll through the project photos**. Seeing the sweater on lots of different body shapes, in different yarns and colors, can make a huge difference in an informed decision!

"But Shelley...I don't want to do all that research. Just tell me what I should make!"

Okay, let's simplify this!

Here are our suggestions for YOU to cast on for the Love Sweaters Challenge, based on where you are on the LoopsLove Success Path.

"I LOVE YARN!"

If you're a newer knitter, and you've never made a sweater, we recommend starting with a baby sweater to give you confidence. Baby sweaters usually have nice, straight lines (just like babies!) and they're quick to make. So you'll develop confidence while you learn the basics of sweater construction.

Pattern suggestions, from fastest to slowest (based on yarn weight):

Quick Oats by Taiga Hilliard Designs
- http://bit.ly/quickoats
Yarn suggestion: Forget-Me-Not 100% cotton
- http://bit.ly/plymouthyarn

Cockleshell Cardigan by Amy Christoffers
- http://bit.ly/cardigan212
Yarn suggestion: Blue Sky Fibers Cotton
- http://bit.ly/bluefiber

Flax Light by Tin Can Knits - http://bit.ly/flax212

Has the added benefit of adult sizes, so you can make a "practice" one in the baby size, then graduate to an adult size!

Yarn suggestion: The Fibre Co. Canopy Fingering - http://bit.ly/canopy212

Julie Dress – crocheted – by Weiyan Huang
Yarn suggestion: Rowan Baby Cashsoft Merino

"I LOVE TO LEARN!"

For the adventurous beginner, or the more advanced knitter who hasn't made a sweater yet, we suggest one of these very do-able, wear-able designs – depending on your personal style preferences.

Flax Light by Tin Can Knits - http://bit.ly/flax212
Yarn suggestion: The Uncommon Thread Posh Fingering - http://bit.ly/thread212

Tumble Cardi by Loops (see index section of this Workbook)
Yarn suggestions:
Berroco Mykonos - http://bit.ly/berroco212
Mykonos Stonewash - http://bit.ly/berroco213
or Summer DK Linen - http://bit.ly/yarns212

Hot Hippie Vest – crocheted – find pattern in index of this Workbook (crochet version is on back)
Yarn suggestion: Woolen Boon BFL Lace

"I LOVE SWEATERS!"

You've already made at least one garment, and you'd like to make one that fits you perfectly – a real piece of everyday clothing that will slide effortlessly into your wardrobe. We highly recommend you experience Amy Herzog's CustomFit sweaters! Inside her brilliantly designed website, Amy takes you through the process of taking ALL your measurements, then the program generates a pattern designed specifically for you!

Two of our favorite CustomFit Designs:

Mine Hill Cardigan by Amy Herzog
- http://bit.ly/cardigan215
Yarn Suggestion: Bigfoot Fibers Silky Yak DK
- http://bit.ly/silkyak

Cushman by Amy Herzog
- http://bit.ly/cushman212
Yarn Suggestion: The Fiber Co. Road to China
Light - http://bit.ly/fibreco212

Not a CustomFit personalize-able pattern, but free:

February Fitted Pullover by Amy Herzog
- http://bit.ly/fitted212
Yarn Suggestion: Araucania Lujoso
http://bit.ly/lujoso212

For crocheters:
The Habitat Cardigan by Jess Coppom
Yarn suggestion: Malabrigo Rios

"I LOVE TO DESIGN!"

Have fun playing with your own textural "strips" to the worsted version of
Joji's beloved Boxy.

Worsted Boxy by Joji Locatelli
- http://bit.ly/boxy212
With textural mods by Shelley Brander (see index
section of this Workbook)
Yarn Suggestion: Juniper Moon Farm Zooey
- http://bit.ly/juniper212

For crocheters:
Mount Tremper Sweater by Alexandra Tavel
You can play around with stripe placement and
add texture to a section or two if you wish!
Yarn suggestion: Malabrigo Rios

"I LOVE MYSELF!"

For more advanced sweater makers, we suggest hopping on the bandwagon
with Mason-Dixon Knitting's "Bang Out A Sweater" knitalong from 2019. You
choose your adventure from Norah Gaughan's designs featured in MDK Field
Guide #9: Revolution. Cardigan or pullover? Short sleeves or long? It's up to
you!

For advanced crocheters:
Check out **Pinecrest Pullover** by Jennifer Ozses
Be sure to swatch first to get the hang of the cluster pattern.
Yarn suggestion: Berroco Modern Cotton

Need help choosing your yarn...
or calculating how much you need?

The Loops Troops are here for you!
Email support@loopslove.com or
call **877-566-7765**.

PART 3

☐ THE JOY OF SWATCHING. NO, REALLY!

Every single designer we've ever met preaches the same sermon: YOU MUST SWATCH.

Seriously, you may be tempted to skip this and cast right on.

But think about it. If your gauge is off by even one stitch, that can translate into 5-10 inches "off" over the circumference of a finished sweater. OUCH!

So we suggest a mindset shift.

Think of swatching as a fun test-drive of the fabric you'll be creating.

You get to know the yarn and how it behaves.

You get to play around with different needle types, and see how they play with the yarn.

So we suggest you embrace your swatch as a fun and relaxing first step. Amy from La Bien Aimée treats herself to "Sunday Swatching." It's important to swatch in your "natural state" – don't try to force your gauge. If you normally knit with a glass of wine, swatch with a glass of wine!

Likewise, you want to swatch like you plan to knit. Use the same needles (circular or straight, wood or metal etc.). And be sure to swatch using the recommended gauge stitch. If it says to swatch in the pattern stitch, do it! Your tension with a purl or pattern stitch may be different that your stockinette tension.

And with swatches, bigger is better.

We like aiming for a swatch that's 6-10" square. Loops Trooper Tracy thinks of her swatch as a big slice of bread – you want to make a swatch so big that you leave all the "crust" – i.e., the edges – and measure just the center. So for example, take the pattern's recommended gauge (for example, 4 stitches per inch) and multiple by 8 inches for your swatch. You would cast on 48 stitches and work until your swatch measures 8 inches from the start.

Then take the all-important, but often skipped, final step. BLOCK YOUR SWATCH. Let it soak in cool or lukewarm water, then lay flat to dry – do not pin it out, that's cheating! :)

Not a fan of pilling or sweaters that stretch out of shape after just one wearing? Use Amy Herzog's "poke test." If you can't poke your finger through your finished swatch fabric, you're good to go! (If you're going for a more "open" fabric, that's okay – just make sure your yarn choice isn't too elastic or stretchy. For example, the Tumble Cardi is knit at a more open gauge, so we chose a strong linen-based yarn that's unlikely to stretch, give or pill.

So I've done my swatch. Now what?
Lay it flat, and use an old-fashioned wooden or metal ruler to count how many stitches you have across the middle 4 inches of your swatch. A "hard" ruler makes it harder to cheat. Do not cheat yourself!

If you have too many stitches, swatch again with a bigger needle.

If you have too few stitches, swatch again with a smaller needle.

"But I don't want to waste my yarn."
We hear this a lot, and we understand. But isn't your time worth more than yarn? And what is your gauge is off, and you "waste" a whole sweater's worth of yarn, plus all that time?

Most designers allow for a generous swatch when calculating their yarn amounts. But if you're still worried, buy that extra skein.

You can use your finished swatch as a coaster for your morning joe. Or if you're really industrious, you can stitch them together and make a baby blanket!

PART 4

NEEDLES, NOTIONS AND RECOMMENDED RESOURCES.

The right needles and tools can make all the difference in your sweater-making happiness, and in your success.

Here's a handy list of the Loops Troops' favorite needles and tools for making sweaters.

- **Circular Needles:**
  You can work flat or tubular (in the round) sweaters, and they're more portable – no poking the person next to you on the plane! We tend to favor the speed and ease of metal-based needles, UNLESS we're working with a slippery fiber like silk or bamboo. Then we opt for wooden needles like bamboo or rosewood.

- **Interchangeable Needle Sets:**
  These save money in the long run, especially for newer knitters. And it's super convenient when you're swatching.

- **Life Lines:**
  Use waste yarn or dental floss to insert a "lifeline" into your knitting, in case you need to rip back. Especially life-saving for lace knitting.

- **Round stitch markers** to distinguish important locations (beginning of round, pattern repeats).

- **Locking stitch markers** are handy for dropped stitches, short rows, row counting and more!

- **Tapestry needles** are crucial for weaving in ends. The bent-tip ones are good to avoid splitting your yarn, and the sharp-tip ones are good for intentionally splitting the yarn to secure it.

- **Soak or Eucalan** – Just say NO to Woolite, which can break down your fine fibers. These no-rinse washes allow your fabric to bloom beautifully during wet blocking.

- **Clover Clips** "make seaming a dream" according to Kay Gardiner from MDK.

- **We love Ann Budd's Handy Gauge Ruler** for an extra visual check of your gauge

- **Row Counter** – There are lots of options on the market. We like the Kacha-Kacha counter, Cocoknits row counter, and the variety of apps available for your mobile devices – since you always have those with you!

- **Journal!** It's so easy to lose track of written patterns. So we like to keep a knitter's journal to jot down any notes or mods.

- **Four of our favorite Sweater-related reads:**
  - » Ultimate Sweater Book by Amy Herzog
  - » Knit Wear Love by Amy Herzog
  - » Cocoknits Sweater Workshop (book) by Julie Weisenberger
  - » The Knitters Book of Yarn by Clara Parkes

PART 5:

☐ FABULOUS FINISHING.

Love it or hate it, finishing is the crucial step that elevates your project from "homemade" to "handmade."

Here are a few golden finishing nuggets from some of our favorite Knit Stars teachers.

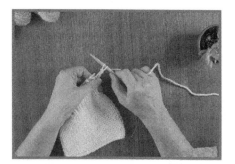

Hannah's easy loose bind-off

Finishing begins with the bind-off! One of the most common mistakes we see at Loops is that people bind off their edges too tightly. This limits your ability to block your sweater pieces. But it can be hard to remember those "stretchy" bind-offs!

Here's a super-easy "stretchy" bind-off method from Hannah Fettig in Knit Stars 1.0.

- When ready to bind off, go up one needle size (for example, from a 10 to 10.5 size needle).

- Tension your yarn a little more loosely than usual.

- Knit two stitches and give them a little tug before pulling first stitch over second stitch to bind off.

- Continue as established until all stitches are bound off.

Blocking with Michele Wang

Blocking is the single most important thing you can do to give your sweater a more professional look. You can wet-block or steam-block, but wet-block usually gives you the most bang for your buck, as the fibers will be most flexible when fully saturated.

Here are the steps:

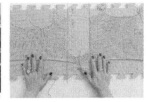

1. Block before seaming your pieces together. Fill a large basin with cool or tepid water and rinseless wool soap, such as Soak. (If you're using a red or bright pink shade, we recommend sticking with cold water here).

2. Hold and press down knitted pieces into the water and keep them submerged (approx. 1 minutes) until they are fully soaked and will stay underwater by themselves. Allow to soak for 15 minutes – 1 hour.

3. Use puzzle piece blocking mats that don't absorb moisture and allow you to customize your blocking mat based on the piece you are blocking.

4. T-pins, blocking wires, and rulers allow you to correctly pin pieces to blocking mat (according to measurements of the pattern schematics). We also really like the Knit Blockers from Knitter's Pride – makes the work faster and easier!

5. Allow to fully dry before un-pinning and seaming – and keep the pets out of your blocking room!

Mattress Stitch with Meghan

In Knit Stars 1.0, Meghan Fernandes did a great demo on how to do the mattress stitch. There are lots of other seaming and grafting options, but this is our go-to for most every situation! Swiftly creates an invisible seam.

1. Leave a tail of yarn (either from the cast-on or bind-off edge) three times the length of the section you'll be seaming. If you don't have a tail available, cut a piece from your yarn cake.

2. Go under the first two "rungs" between the first and second column of stitches on the left side, and pull up your strand.

3. Repeat on the right side of your work, and draw up on the yarn to pull the pieces together – not too tightly.

4. Continue to work back and forth – two rungs from the left side, then two from the right, until the section has been seamed.

5. Weave in your ends.

ACTION ITEM:

☐ Post your finished sweater in the LoopsLove Challenge Facebook group. We can't wait to see it! Bonus points for wearing it and posting a selfie!

CONGRATULATIONS! You finished your sweater. Now it's time to treat yourself to a little self-care with our bonus challenge, Love Your Self.

Hot Hippie Vest

YARN:	TOOLS:	GAUGE:
2 "superskeins" Koigu Lace, 440 yards each, complementary colors	Crochet: I/5.5mm hook; Knit: #8 32" or size needed to obtain gauge	Knit: 14.5 sts = 4"; Crochet: 8 rows = 4", 3 DC groups + 2 spaces = 4"

KNIT VERSION

Finished measurements: 30" from neck to bottom of back, armholes 11" deep

Notes: It is very important to work a gauge swatch with this project. Wet-block your swatch before measuring for gauge. If you have too many stitches, try a bigger needle size. If you have too few, try a smaller needle size.

OPTIONAL EYELET ROWS

We added an eyelet row after the *first* 20 rows and again before the *last* 20 rows, as follows:
k6, *yo, k2tog* to last 6 sts, k6
If you choose to do this, be sure work your eyelet rows on right-side rows, and keep in mind you will have to watch your yarn usage more closely, to be sure you place your second eyelet row and still have yarn to finish 20 rows plus bind-off.

ONCE YOU HAVE THE CORRECT GAUGE, START KNITTING:

With your first color (your choice), cast on 90 stitches and work in stockinette stitch (*knit a row, purl a row* repeat) until work measures 30" from cast-on or you run out of yarn, Hot Hippie Vest whichever comes first, ending at end of row. Make note of your length to this point and attach a clip-on marker or safety pin. Attach second skein/color and continue in stockinette to the same length as your first color. Bind off very loosely (we always recommend going up two needle sizes for a loose bind-off). Wet block piece to 30" wide by 60" long.

To assemble (see diagram below):

Fold piece in half so that cast-on and bind-off edges are touching and the fold line is on the left. Sew caston and bind-off edge from A to B for a 3.5" seam. Next, reposition the piece so that the A-to-B seam is in the center. Bring point A to point C, which is where you changed colors and clipped on your marker. Clip point A to point C. Now, seam 6" from C to D, and 6" from C to E, for a total back seam length of 12" - this completes your vest!

KNIT VEST ASSEMBLY DIAGRAM:

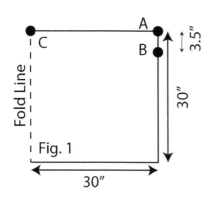

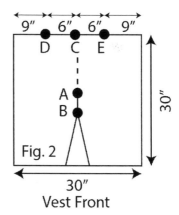

CROCHET VERSION:

Finished sizes: Small: 20" x 44" Medium: 24" x 54" Large: 28" x 64"

INSTRUCTIONS: Worked from bottom up for sizes S (M, L)

With darker color, chain 150 (165, 180) stitches.

Row 1: DC in 4th ch from hook, 1 DC in next chain, Ch 2, skip next 2 chains, *DC in next 3 chains, Ch 2, skip next 2 chains*, repeat from *to* 28 (31, 34) more times, ending with 3 DC. Ch 5 turn. (30, 33, 36 groups of 3 DC)

Row 2: *3 DC in next Ch 2 space, Ch 2*, repeat from *to* 28 (31, 34) more times. 1 DC in last DC of row. (Ch 3 at the end of previous row counts as 1 DC.) Ch 3, turn. (29, 32, 35 groups of 3 DC)

Row 3: 2 DC in first Ch 2 space, *Ch 2, 3 DC in next Ch 2 space* repeat from *to* to end of row ending with 3 DC, Ch 5, turn. (30, 33, 36 groups of 3 DC)

Repeat rows 2 and 3 four (seven, nine) more times, then work row 2 one more time. You should now have 12 (18, 22) rows. Break yarn and attach lighter color yarn, Ch 3, turn. Next row will be row 13 (19, 23) and the start of front left half of vest ("vest piece").

VEST PIECE:

Row 13 (19, 23): With lighter color yarn, 2 DC in Ch 2 space, *Ch 2, 3 DC in next Ch 2 space*, repeat from *to* until you have 9 (10, 11) groups of 3 DC, Ch 2, 1 DC in next Ch 2 space, Ch 3 turn.

Row 14 (20, 24): 2 DC in first Ch 2 space, *Ch 2, 3 DC in next Ch 2 space* repeat from *to* until you have 9 (10, 11) groups of 3 DCs, Ch 2, 1 DC in last DC, Ch 3, turn.

Row 15 (21, 25): 2 DC in Ch 2 space, *Ch 2, 3 DC in next Ch 2 space* repeat from *to* until you have 9 (10, 11) groups of 3 DC, Ch 2, 1 DC in last DC of row, Ch 3 turn.

Repeat rows 14 & 15 (20 & 21, 24 & 25) two (three, four) more times, break off yarn.

For second Vest Piece, at opposite end of vest, attach lighter color yarn to 1st Ch 5 space at beginning of Row 12 (18, 22), Ch 3.

Repeat Vest Piece instructions. Break off yarn.

Once both left and right halves of the vest are done, begin to work on the center piece of the vest (which is the back of the vest).

VEST BACK:

Start between left and right front pieces, (doesn't matter which end), as follows:

Row 13 (19, 23): Attach lighter color yarn between left and right front pieces at Ch 2 space where there is one DC from side panel.

Ch 5, *3 DC in next Ch 2 space, Ch 2* repeat * until you have 10 (11, 12) groups of 3 DC, Ch 2, 1 DC in next Ch 2 space (at this point you should meet up with Ch 2 space with 1 DC from beginning of front piece), Ch 3 turn.

Row 14 (20, 24:) 2 DC in Ch 2 space, *Ch 2, 3 DC in next Ch 2 space* repeat from *to* until you have 11(12, 13) groups of 3 DC, Ch 5 turn.

Row 15 (21, 25:) *3 DC in next Ch 2 space, Ch 2* repeat from *to* until you have 10(11, 12) groups of 3 DC, Ch 2, 1 DC last DC of row, Ch 5, turn.

Repeat rows 14 & 15 (20 & 21, 24 & 25) two (three, four) times, break off yarn.

Row 20 (28, 34): Attach yarn at outer edge of right front piece. Ch 5, *3 DC in next Ch 2 space, Ch 2* repeat from *to* to end of row. At the end of front piece, Ch 2, continue row on back piece by 3 DC in 1st Ch 5 space of back piece. Continue with pattern of (3 DC in Ch 2 spaces, Ch 2) until you come to the end of back piece, attach left front piece in the same fashion as right piece.

Continue in pattern of (3 DC in Ch 2 spaces, Ch 2) until end of row, Ch 2, 1 DC in last DC of row, Ch 3 turn.

Row 21(29, 35): 2 DC in Ch 2 space, *Ch 2, 3 DC in Ch 2 space* repeat from *to* to end of row ending with 3 DC, Ch 5, turn.

(Note: each armhole counts as a Ch 2 space.)

Row 22 (30, 36): *3 DC in next Ch 2 space, Ch 2* repeat from *to* to end of row.

Repeat rows 21 & 22 (29 & 30, 35 & 36) four more times, then repeat row 21 (29, 35) one more time. At the end of row, bind off yarn and weave in tail.

Total Rows: 31(39, 45) Steam block, wear and enjoy.

Tumble Cardi

A LOOPS ORIGINAL

YARN:	TOOLS:	GAUGE:
4 skeins (1080 yards) Euroflax Sport (one size fits most)	#7 needles	4.5 sts and 6 rows = 1 inch (after washing and drying)

This lovely linen cardigan gets even softer and drapey-er after a spin through your washer a tumble in your dryer!

CABLE TWIST PATTERN:

Rows 1, 3, 5, 7, 9, 11, 13, 17, 19, 21, 23, 25, 29: Knit

Row 2 and all even rows: Purl

Row 15: Knit 4, *slip next 3 sts onto cable needle and hold in back of work, knit next 3 sts then knit 3 sts from cable needle, knit 6* repeat from * across row.

Row 31: Knit 10, *slip next 3 sts onto cable needle and hold in back of work, knit next 3 sts then knit 3 sts from cable needle, knit 6* repeat from * across row.

RIGHT SLEEVE, BACK AND LEFT SLEEVE:

Cast on 28 sts. Starting with Row 1 of cable pattern, work 8 rows. Maintaining pattern, increase 1 st at end of next row and every following 4th row until you have 34 sts. Then increase 1 st at end of every other row until you have 48 sts.

Work even until sleeve measures 9", ending with a right side (RS) row. As you increase sts, work the cable pattern into the increased sts.

Next row (WS): Cast on 60 sts, place marker (PM), cast on 6 sts (these sts will be kept in k1, p1 rib for the entire length of back) - 114 sts total.

Next row: (p1, k1) 3x, slip marker, purl to end of row. Continuing with pattern, work across back until it measures 20" (29" total from start), ending with a RS row. Bind off 66 sts, purl to end. Decrease 1 st at end of every other row until you have 34 sts, then every 4th row until you have 28 sts. Work 8 rows stockinette. Bind off.

LEFT SLEEVE AND LEFT FRONT:

Work as for back until front measures 14" (23" total). Bind off.

RIGHT SLEEVE AND RIGHT FRONT:

Work as for back except increases will be done at beginning of row and cast-on will be done at beginning of right side row as well.

COLLAR:

On back, measure the center 7.5", placing markers. Pick up 28 sts between markers.

WS: Purl 1 row

RS: Cable twist row: k5, cable twist over next 6 sts, k6, cable twist over next 6 sts, k5.

Work 15 rows in stockinette st.

Next row: k11, work cable twist over next 6 sts, k11.

Purl 1 row, knit 1 row, purl 1 row. Bind off.

FINISHING:

Pin fronts and back together along shoulders, bringing the fronts up to meet collar on back (see diagram). Seam using mattress stitch. Sew underarm and side seams using mattress stitch. Machine wash and dry your finished garment. Iron if you choose.

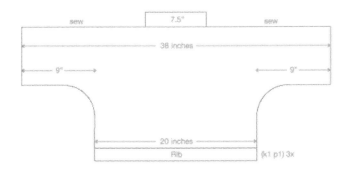

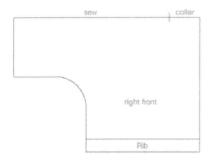

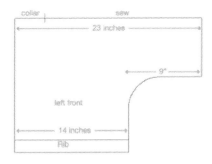

Aprés-Tennis Sweater

OUR MODS FOR A LACE VERSION OF JOJI'S "WORSTED BOXY" SWEATER

YARN:	TOOLS:	GAUGE:
Juniper Moon Farm Zooey. 5 skeins	#9 US needles	4.5 sts = 1 inch in stockinette st

This piece was inspired by pooki's Lace Boxy on ravelry, which was inspired by Joji's Worsted Boxy and Erin Kate Archer's Cancun Boxy Lace Top. Start by buying and downloading "Worsted Boxy" by Joji Locatelli from Ravelry. I made the Small.

K1, P1 for 5 rounds.

Work garter st for 9 rounds, starting and ending with P row.

Work Mesh Stitch Section as follows:
Row 1: Knit
Rows 2, 4 and 6 (WS): Purl
Row 3 (RS): K1, *YO, sl1 knitwise, k2, psso* repeat from * to last 2 sts, k2
Row 5 (RS): *YO, sl1 knitwise, k2 sts and pass slipped st over them
Row 7 (RS): K2, *YO, sl1knitwise, k2, psso*

Repeat Mesh Stitch Section once more.

Work in stockinette (knit) for 8 rounds.
Work 12 rounds Net Stitch as follows:
k1, *YO, k2tog* repeat from * to last st, k1.
Purl 1 round.
Work in stockinette (knit) 8 rounds.

Work Bobble Row: K19, make bobble, repeat to end of row.
To make bobble: kfb, kfb, k all in the same stitch, then turn work over to WS
and purl back across these 5 new sts, then turn work back to right side and
cast off 4 sts, knitting the 5th stitch.

Work in stockinette (knit) 8 rounds
Purl 1 round.

Work Crossed Dropstitch Section as follows:
Rows 1-4: Knit
Row 5: K1, knit to last st, wrapping yarn 3 times around needle for each st, k1
Row 6: *Sl8 sts, dropping all extra wraps, forming 8 long sts on RH needle,
insert LH needle into 4 long sts furthest from RH needle tip and pass them
over the 4 long sts closest to RH needle tip, return all sts to LH needle and k8
in this new orientation; rep from * to end.

Work in stockinette (knit) 5 rounds.
Purl 1 round

Repeat Mesh Stitch Section 3 times.

Work in stockinette (knit) 5 rounds.

Work 6 rounds Net Stitch.

From this point on, continue working in Stockinette Stitch and follow
instructions for seamless version of Worsted Boxy - divide work for armholes,
work front and back, shape shoulders, neckband, sleeves etc.

CHAPTER 6:

The Love Your Self Challenge

Time for a break!

So much to remember during the holiday season!

What's the one thing we always forget?

Ourselves.

We're so busy making, baking and taking care of everyone else, we forget to make time for ME.

That's what the next 30 days are all about. Taking time to rest our tired hands and heads and feet, kicking back and nurturing all of our senses.

It's perfect during the holidays, or anytime you've just emerged from a particularly stressful season.

This one is just for you.

Enjoy!

☐ SEE AND TOUCH.

Years ago, I read a beautiful essay – I think it was in a Rowan newsletter, and I've long since lost it, unfortunately.

But I remember the idea. And it was so beautifully simple, I want to pass it on to you.

It's called a "Seeds of Intention" scarf.

You choose someone close to you, who is going through a particularly rough patch. Maybe it's illness, or relationship trouble, or teenage angst, or loss.

You choose a beautiful yarn that you know they would love. Something very simple and smooth and soft. For the color, you might choose white, cream or a very light grey – something that won't distract you from the process or cause other emotions to cloud your thoughts.

Then you make a very simple seed stitch scarf.

Why seed stitch? Because it is slow. By the very fact that you have to move the yarn from front to back, back to front, it forces you to slow down.

It also requires no memorization. There's no pattern to reference. You can focus entirely on the stitches. If you get lost, you can always just remember this seed stitch mantra: "knit the purls, purl the knits."

As you sit down to work on your scarf, set an intention for the person for whom you are making it. It might be a phrase like "may you have peace" or "may you be well." Or it might be just a single word, like "love."

As you are working on the scarf, hold this intention in your mind and heart.

When you complete it, gift it to your intended. Share the intention you have for them, either in person or in a card.

And yes, it's ok for the intended to be you :)

I think it's a nice idea to have one of these scarves on your needles all the time.

Now here is a simple "recipe" for a KNIT seed stitch scarf.

First, choose your yarn weight and needles that are about 2 sizes larger than what is called for on the ballband.

To make approximately a 7-inch-wide scarf:
> For fingering yarn: Cast on 45 stitches on #4 needles.
> For sportweight yarn: Cast on 39 stitches with #6 needles.
> For DK weight yarn: Cast on 35 stitches with #8 needles.
> For worsted weight yarn: Cast on 29 stitches with #10 needles.
> For chunky weight yarn: Cast on 21 stitches on #13 needles.
> For bulky weight yarn: Cast on 15 stitches on #17 needles.

Now, just work *K1, P1* every row until you are done. Bind off loosely.

You can sew the ends together to make a cowl if you like.

If you decide to work in the round, you'll want to cast on an odd number of stitches, join in the round and place a marker. Then alternate rounds of *K1, P1* with rounds of *P1, K1* - again, you're always knitting the purl stitches, and purling the knit stitches.

Here's a simple "recipe" for a CROCHETED seed stitch scarf

1. Start with a chain.

2. Double crochet in the next stitch.

3. Single crochet in the next stitch.

4. Repeat steps 2 and 3 across the row.

5. At the end of the row, turn...

6. Continue across the row, alternating by making a single crochet in the double crochet of the previous row, and vice versa.

If you're someone who really needs a printed pattern, or wants something just a tiny bit more complex, check out:

GAP-tastic Cowl Pattern by Jen Geigley
http://bit.ly/cowl212

Guy by Kim Hargreaves
http://bit.ly/guybykim

Palace Moss Cowl by Shelley Brander on the LoopsLove free pattern page
http://bit.ly/patterns-knitters

Seed Stitch Cowl by Katya Novikova (crochet) http://bit.ly/seedstitchbykatya

☐ LISTEN.

For the next 30 days, take time to listen to something new and different, something that feeds your soul and inspires you.

To Listen to while you stitch.

Lucky for us knitters and crocheters, we are great at multi-tasking! So we can listen to audiobooks while we stitch.

Three of my favorite audiobooks for listening to while knitting are:

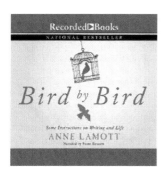

1. *Bird by Bird: Some Instructions on Writing and Life* by Anne Lamott.

    This book has inspired me to write my own book! Anne believes everyone has a book inside of them. She'll help you find your passion and your voice. But even if you have no desire to write a book, you'll love listening to Anne's warm, witty words, spoken by Susan Bennett.

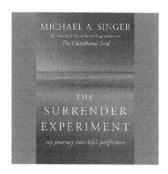

2. *The Surrender Experiment: My Journey into Life's Perfection* by Michael A. Singer. Narrated by the author, this book blew my mind. I thought it was a business book, but it turns out to be a true-life story about what happens when you just let go. I listened to it while flying to a conference, decided to put it into practice while at the conference, and was astounded at the magical moments that followed. We knitters and crocheters tend to like to control our outcomes... so I think all of us can benefit from this message.

3. *A Stash of One's Own* by Clara Parkes. This compendium of tales from 21 knitters will help you feel better about your stash and all things yarn! Named one of the top 10 lifestyle books for fall 2017 by Publishers Weekly.

To listen to NOT while you stitch.

With the rapid growth of Loops and Knit Stars, and all the associated traveling, I've had to really work hard at establishing some self-care routines. And the one that's made the biggest difference is meditation.

I resisted this for a long time. I had this misperception that meditation was "woo-woo," something that only yogis and vegans do. But I could not have been more wrong! In fact, I've come to realize that knitting and crocheting is a form of meditation – and I LOVE KNITTING! It turns out, I dig meditation too.

What made the difference for me was the app "Simple Habit."

It's a really cool, user-friendly app with thousands of meditations from a ton of different teachers. It's organized to guide you through all sorts of situations, everything from "Before you fly" to "Resiliency" to "Public Speaking."

There's a free version of the app and a paid version.

My favorite series on the free version is "Thought Detox."

My favorites on the paid version are:
"Living Your Truth" and "Manifest Your Dreams" by Sean M. Kelly – amazing!
"30 Days to Better Sleep" by Cory Muscara – it works!
"Start Your Day with Gratitude" by Cory Muscara – we could all use more of this :)

Resist the urge to knit while you do meditate...just relax and enjoy.

☐ SMELL AND TASTE

Another big self-care discovery for me this year is essential oils. At first, I thought I was late to the party, but it turns out there are lots of people who have yet to discover them!

My friend Lisa starting using (then selling) Young Living essential oils and yes, they are the best of the best! But there are lots of great alternatives such as DoTerra oils and others that are readily available on Amazon or at your local superstore.

Here are some of my favorite essential oil combinations and tips from the past year. Treat yourself! And these make great gifts if you're running short on gift-knitting time. Note: Spray bottles and rollers are available on Amazon.com.

1. Lavender for better sleep
- Combine 20 drops lavender with a carrier oil in a roller bottle and rub a little into the bottoms of your feet before bedtime.
- Diffuse 4 drops lavender + 4 drops Stress Away at bedtime
- Combine 5 drops lavender + 5 drops cedarwood + 2tsp witch hazel or vodka in a 2- or 3-oz spray bottle. Fill to top with distilled water, shake to combine. Spray on your pillow before bedtime.
- Sprinkle a few drops of lavender into a hot bath before bed.

2. Uplifting combinations for daytime focus
- Lavender + lime in the diffuser
- Peppermint + lemon in the diffuser
- Either of the above in a spray bottle for a room spray

3. "Poo-pourri" Spray a.k.a. #2 spray ;-)

- Combine 4 drops lemon + 4 drops peppermint + 4 drops eucalyptus + 2tsp witch hazel or vodka + distilled water to fill 2- or 3-oz spray bottle. Shake to combine. Spray into toilet bowl BEFORE you go.

4. Holiday "Hot Wassail" spray

- 15 drops citrus + 4 drops cinnamon + 2 drops clove + 2tsp witch hazel + distilled water to fill 2- or 3-oz spray bottle. Shake to combine. Spray to fill room with holiday scent.

5. Other great oil combinations...

- Northern Lights Black Spruce + Bergamot (promotes restfulness)
- Lavender + Peppermint + Eucalyptus + Ylang Ylang (PMS)
- Ylang Ylang + Lavender + German Chamomile (floral body spray)

You can also add flavor with essential oils – if labeled for this use!

- I love adding a drop of lemon, orange or lime to a bottle of water to give it a flavor boost.
- Add a drop of lavender to a martini
- Add a drop of peppermint to chocolate cookies

SCHEDULE IT!

Use your phone calendar or even purchase a printed calendar and dedicate it to scheduling time for YOU, every day! Some ideas:

- Treat yourself to a new audiobook
- Indulge in a new bath bomb
- Go for a long walk with an old friend you haven't seen in awhile
- Make a new playlist to stitch to
- Pay for someone's order behind you in the drive-through
- Try a new soup recipe in a slow cooker; pick up some crusty bread on the way home
- Go to your favorite coffee shop and knit
- Go out to breakfast and linger over coffee or tea
- Get a free makeover at a department store or beauty store
- Make a natural scrub from brown sugar, olive oil and essential oils and exfoliate the day away!
- Do a gratitude meditation
- Share a bottle of wine with someone who least expects it
- Spend the entire day in bed, devouring a new book
- Subscribe to a fun new magazine (like Laine or Pom Pom Quarterly)
- Make a fruit crisp for dessert tonight, just because!
- Give your hair a homemade hot oil treatment (check Pinterest for recipes)
- Buy yourself a fresh bouquet of flowers
- Treat yourself to a fun set of stitch markers or new project bag
- Try a new cookie recipe and fill up the cookie jar for the week
- Take a new yoga class – maybe aerial yoga?

With Special Thanks...

- To Brent, my husband, who let me pursue this crazy dream of opening a yarn store, even thought we were in the midst of managing a chaotic branding business and an equally chaotic home with three small kids.

- To my now-grown kids, Sam, Cecily and Mallory, who spent countless hours in the Loops back room while I shelved yarn in the early days.

- To my mother-in-law, Jean Brander, who told Brent "You can never let her close that yarn business - it makes her too happy."

- To the late Walt Helmerich, who took a chance and leased me the first store space (after I knit him a cashmere scarf :)

- To the Loops Troops, especially Tracy for contributing to the content and Ruth for proofreading...I am so, so lucky to "work" alongside the nicest, most creative people on the planet.

- And most of all, to our amazing customers around the world, who have made our communities - both in-store and online - the ultra-positive, supportive, creative spaces that I always longed for as a younger knitter.

The Loops Love Movement

Here's what we stand for:

Lose the negativity   ⟫⟶⟶   Find the positivity

Lose the criticism   ⟫⟶⟶   Find the fun

Lose the disappointment   ⟫⟶⟶   Find the empowerment

Lose the fear   ⟫⟶⟶   Find the love!

Share your progress on your own social media.
Use #loopslovechallenge and be sure to mention @loops (Facebook)
and @loopslove (Instagram) so we can see your posts!

LoopsLove.com
Loops, a yarn store
6034 S. Yale
Tulsa, OK 74135

Facebook:
/Loops

Instagram:
@loopslove

Ravelry group:
Loopalicious

Join the LoopsLove Challenge group at LoopsMembers.com

Check out our on-trend, effortless yarn club
subscription at LoopsMembers.com

Discover the inspiration, learning and community of KnitStars.com

Made in the USA
Columbia, SC
27 July 2019